An Affirmation Away

DAILY AFFIRMATION JOURNAL

ALICIA HENSON

AN AFFIRMATION AWAY

COPYRIGHT© 2021 BY ALICIA HENSON

ISBN: 9780578874074
ISBN: 9780578874081

PRINTED IN THE UNITED STATES OF AMERICA

PUBLISHER: JOSEPH'S MINISTRY, LLC
            WWW.JOSEPHSMINISTRYLLC.COM

Acknowledgments

A very special thank you to God, my Father, who gave me the idea of writing this affirmation journal/planner. The biggest lesson He has taught me along my journey is to never let my faith waiver. As long as I trust in Him, no matter the circumstance, everything will always fall into its proper place.

I humbly extend my thanks to my pastors Michael and Natalie Todd for allowing God to lead them in ways I could not have imagined. Because of their obedience, they have allowed me to rededicate my life to Christ on August 25, 2019.

My deepest gratitude for my brother and sister in Christ, Ryan and Jalisa Green, are beyond words. These two introduced me to one of Pastor Michael Todd's popular sermon series "Relationship Goals." They were the cause of the progression of my walk in Christ.

Family is everything to me. My oldest brother and mentor, Carlos A. Henson (also known as "The Prospective Changer"), has had a front row seat to both the hard and prime times of my life. I can't express my gratitude enough for the many lessons he has taught me. He has helped strengthen my walk with Christ and it will only get stronger from here.

I give all credit to Ms. Keena Jones-Williams, who introduced me to journaling. I made a visit to The Arkansas Federal Credit Union in September of 2018, and she mentioned that I should purchase a journal to write out my thoughts.

Last, but certainly not least, this would not be possible without my gracious pharmacy manager, Ana Pahlevanyan. I tremendously appreciate her passionate encouragement and selfless heart.

About the Author

Alicia L. Henson is the daughter of Clifton Henson Jr. and Vivian L. Stewart. She was born and raised in Little Rock, AR. On June 29, 2019, she stepped out in faith and moved to Tulsa, OK to join Transformation Church (pastors Michael and Natalie Todd). Her siblings consist of 5 brothers, and 2 sisters; she also has 7 nieces and 2 nephews. She is currently a Senior Certified Pharmacy Technician at Walgreens. Alicia is still pursuing her education to become a physician assistant, but she has received her Associate of Science in Liberal Arts and Sciences degree from the University of Arkansas-Pulaski Technical College. She enjoys traveling, spending time with family and friends, and attending church.

This Journal Belongs To:

Monthly PLANNER

JAN FEB MAR APR MAY JUN

SUN	MON	TUE	WED

JUL   OCT

AUG   NOV

SEP   DEC YEAR ______________

<u>Worship Song of the Month</u>
"Big" by Pastor Mike Jr.

THU	FRI	SAT	NOTES

"I am worthy."

DAILY GOALS

DAILY TASKS

$$\text{``} \mathcal{I} \text{ am loved."}$$

DAILY GOALS

DAILY TASKS

"I am beautiful
inside and out."

DAILY GOALS

DAILY TASKS

"I am a child of God."

DAILY GOALS

DAILY TASKS

DAILY GOALS

DAILY TASKS

"I am protected."

DAILY GOALS

DAILY TASKS

"I am healed."

Self-Care Saturday

CHECK THE BOXES OF THE ACTIVITIES YOU DO TO TAKE CARE OF YOURSELF.

- ☐ EAT THREE MAIN MEALS
- ☐ GO ON A 24-HOUR SOCIAL MEDIA DETOX
- ☐ FIND A QUIET SPOT TO MEDITATE
- ☐ LIGHT AN AROMATIC CANDLE
- ☐ DO A GRATITUDE LIST
- ☐ PRACTICE DEEP BREATHING
- ☐ LISTEN TO GOOD MUSIC
- ☐ EXERCISE
- ☐ CATCH UP WITH A FRIEND
- ☐ VISIT A FAMILY MEMBER
- ☐ SPEND TIME OUTDOORS
- ☐ HAVE A MINI PAMPER SESSION
- ☐ CUDDLE A PET
- ☐ TRY SOMETHING NEW
- ☐ READ A BOOK

Make it a habit to take care of yourself!

THIS WEEK
I AM GRATEFUL FOR

"There is absolutely nothing to worry about."

____

____

____

____

____

____

____

DAILY GOALS

DAILY TASKS

"I have good communication skills."

"Nothing and no one will ruin my day."

DAILY GOALS

DAILY TASKS

"I have self control."

DAILY GOALS

DAILY TASKS

"I am blessed!"

"I am here for a
purpose, on purpose."

DAILY GOALS

DAILY TASKS

Self-Care Saturday

CHECK THE BOXES OF THE ACTIVITIES YOU DO TO TAKE CARE OF YOURSELF.

- ☐ EAT THREE MAIN MEALS
- ☐ GO ON A 24-HOUR SOCIAL MEDIA DETOX
- ☐ FIND A QUIET SPOT TO MEDITATE
- ☐ LIGHT AN AROMATIC CANDLE
- ☐ DO A GRATITUDE LIST
- ☐ PRACTICE DEEP BREATHING
- ☐ LISTEN TO GOOD MUSIC
- ☐ EXERCISE
- ☐ CATCH UP WITH A FRIEND
- ☐ VISIT A FAMILY MEMBER
- ☐ SPEND TIME OUTDOORS
- ☐ HAVE A MINI PAMPER SESSION
- ☐ CUDDLE A PET
- ☐ TRY SOMETHING NEW
- ☐ READ A BOOK

Make it a habit to take care of yourself!

THIS WEEK

I AM GRATEFUL FOR

DAILY GOALS

DAILY TASKS

"I am a leader."

"I am grateful."

DAILY GOALS

DAILY TASKS

"I give it all or nothing!"

"I am 100% healthy."

DAILY GOALS

DAILY TASKS

"*I am teachable.*"

DAILY GOALS

DAILY TASKS

"I am confident in who God has created me to be."

____

____

____

____

____

____

____

DAILY GOALS

○
○
○

DAILY TASKS

○
○
○

Self-Care Saturday

CHECK THE BOXES OF THE ACTIVITIES YOU DO TO TAKE CARE OF YOURSELF.

- ⬭ EAT THREE MAIN MEALS
- ⬭ GO ON A 24-HOUR SOCIAL MEDIA DETOX
- ⬭ FIND A QUIET SPOT TO MEDITATE
- ⬭ LIGHT AN AROMATIC CANDLE
- ⬭ DO A GRATITUDE LIST
- ⬭ PRACTICE DEEP BREATHING
- ⬭ LISTEN TO GOOD MUSIC
- ⬭ EXERCISE
- ⬭ CATCH UP WITH A FRIEND
- ⬭ VISIT A FAMILY MEMBER
- ⬭ SPEND TIME OUTDOORS
- ⬭ HAVE A MINI PAMPER SESSION
- ⬭ CUDDLE A PET
- ⬭ TRY SOMETHING NEW
- ⬭ READ A BOOK

Make it a habit to take care of yourself!

THIS WEEK

I AM GRATEFUL FOR

"I am confident in the things I do and say."

DAILY GOALS

DAILY TASKS

"I retain the things that I learn."

"I am intelligent."

"I surrender my life to God."

____

____

____

____

____

____

____

DAILY GOALS

○
○○
○

DAILY TASKS

○
○○
○

"I am faithful."

"I am selfless."

"I expect nothing, but I appreciate everything."

DAILY GOALS

DAILY TASKS

Self-Care Saturday

CHECK THE BOXES OF THE ACTIVITIES YOU DO TO TAKE CARE OF YOURSELF.

- ☐ EAT THREE MAIN MEALS
- ☐ GO ON A 24-HOUR SOCIAL MEDIA DETOX
- ☐ FIND A QUIET SPOT TO MEDITATE
- ☐ LIGHT AN AROMATIC CANDLE
- ☐ DO A GRATITUDE LIST
- ☐ PRACTICE DEEP BREATHING
- ☐ LISTEN TO GOOD MUSIC
- ☐ EXERCISE
- ☐ CATCH UP WITH A FRIEND
- ☐ VISIT A FAMILY MEMBER
- ☐ SPEND TIME OUTDOORS
- ☐ HAVE A MINI PAMPER SESSION
- ☐ CUDDLE A PET
- ☐ TRY SOMETHING NEW
- ☐ READ A BOOK

Make it a habit to take care of yourself!

THIS WEEK

I AM GRATEFUL FOR

"It is ok not to be ok."

DAILY GOALS

DAILY TASKS

"I am healed from past experiences and situations."

DAILY GOALS

DAILY TASKS

"It is ok to say 'no' to things
I do not agree with."

Hebrews 11:1 (NLT)-"Faith shows the reality of what we hope for; it is the evidence of what we cannot see."

JAN

FEB

MAR

Monthly PLANNER

APR

MAY

JUN

SUN	MON	TUE	WED

<u>Worship Song of the Month</u>
"Relationship Goals"
by Mike Todd

THU	FRI	SAT	NOTES

"I am led by the Holy Spirit."

DAILY GOALS

DAILY TASKS

"*I live each day
with no regrets.*"

DAILY GOALS

DAILY TASKS

DAILY GOALS

DAILY TASKS

"I forgive
(insert their name(s))."

DAILY GOALS

DAILY TASKS

DAILY GOALS

DAILY TASKS

____

____

____

____

____

____

____

DAILY GOALS

DAILY TASKS

Self-Care Saturday

CHECK THE BOXES OF THE ACTIVITIES YOU DO TO TAKE CARE OF YOURSELF.

- ☐ EAT THREE MAIN MEALS
- ☐ GO ON A 24-HOUR SOCIAL MEDIA DETOX
- ☐ FIND A QUIET SPOT TO MEDITATE
- ☐ LIGHT AN AROMATIC CANDLE
- ☐ DO A GRATITUDE LIST
- ☐ PRACTICE DEEP BREATHING
- ☐ LISTEN TO GOOD MUSIC
- ☐ EXERCISE
- ☐ CATCH UP WITH A FRIEND
- ☐ VISIT A FAMILY MEMBER
- ☐ SPEND TIME OUTDOORS
- ☐ HAVE A MINI PAMPER SESSION
- ☐ CUDDLE A PET
- ☐ TRY SOMETHING NEW
- ☐ READ A BOOK

Make it a habit to take care of yourself!

THIS WEEK

I AM GRATEFUL FOR

____

"My flesh is not in charge."

____

____

____

____

____

____

____

____

DAILY GOALS

○

○

○

DAILY TASKS

○

○

○

"I am courageous."

DAILY GOALS

DAILY TASKS

"I am set apart."

"I am a masterpiece."

____

"I am chosen."

____

____

____

____

____

____

____

____

DAILY GOALS

DAILY TASKS

"I am anointed."

____

"I am victorious."

____

____

____

____

____

____

____

____

____

DAILY GOALS

DAILY TASKS

Self-Care Saturday

CHECK THE BOXES OF THE ACTIVITIES YOU DO TO TAKE CARE OF YOURSELF.

- ◯ EAT THREE MAIN MEALS
- ◯ GO ON A 24-HOUR SOCIAL MEDIA DETOX
- ◯ FIND A QUIET SPOT TO MEDITATE
- ◯ LIGHT AN AROMATIC CANDLE
- ◯ DO A GRATITUDE LIST
- ◯ PRACTICE DEEP BREATHING
- ◯ LISTEN TO GOOD MUSIC
- ◯ EXERCISE
- ◯ CATCH UP WITH A FRIEND
- ◯ VISIT A FAMILY MEMBER
- ◯ SPEND TIME OUTDOORS
- ◯ HAVE A MINI PAMPER SESSION
- ◯ CUDDLE A PET
- ◯ TRY SOMETHING NEW
- ◯ READ A BOOK

Make it a habit to take care of yourself!

THIS WEEK

I AM GRATEFUL FOR

"I am holy."

"I am free."

"I am secure."

____

"I am unstoppable."

____

____

____

____

____

____

____

____

DAILY GOALS

_____________________________________ ○
_____________________________________ ○
_____________________________________ ○

DAILY TASKS

_____________________________________ ○
_____________________________________ ○
_____________________________________ ○

"I am called."

"I am a temple."

DAILY GOALS

DAILY TASKS

"I am pure."

Self-Care Saturday

CHECK THE BOXES OF THE ACTIVITIES YOU DO TO TAKE CARE OF YOURSELF.

- ☐ EAT THREE MAIN MEALS
- ☐ GO ON A 24-HOUR SOCIAL MEDIA DETOX
- ☐ FIND A QUIET SPOT TO MEDITATE
- ☐ LIGHT AN AROMATIC CANDLE
- ☐ DO A GRATITUDE LIST
- ☐ PRACTICE DEEP BREATHING
- ☐ LISTEN TO GOOD MUSIC
- ☐ EXERCISE
- ☐ CATCH UP WITH A FRIEND
- ☐ VISIT A FAMILY MEMBER
- ☐ SPEND TIME OUTDOORS
- ☐ HAVE A MINI PAMPER SESSION
- ☐ CUDDLE A PET
- ☐ TRY SOMETHING NEW
- ☐ READ A BOOK

Make it a habit to take care of yourself!

THIS WEEK

I AM GRATEFUL FOR

"I am who God says I am."

DAILY GOALS

DAILY TASKS

"I am redeemed."

"I am content."

"I am mindful of what I say and how I say it."

DAILY GOALS

DAILY TASKS

> *"I am my biggest fan. I am always rooting for me."*

DAILY GOALS

DAILY TASKS

"Things that people say/think about me does not define who I am."

"I am stronger."

DAILY GOALS

DAILY TASKS

Self-Care Saturday

**CHECK THE BOXES OF THE ACTIVITIES
YOU DO TO TAKE CARE OF YOURSELF.**

- ◻ EAT THREE MAIN MEALS
- ◻ GO ON A 24-HOUR SOCIAL MEDIA DETOX
- ◻ FIND A QUIET SPOT TO MEDITATE
- ◻ LIGHT AN AROMATIC CANDLE
- ◻ DO A GRATITUDE LIST
- ◻ PRACTICE DEEP BREATHING
- ◻ LISTEN TO GOOD MUSIC
- ◻ EXERCISE
- ◻ CATCH UP WITH A FRIEND
- ◻ VISIT A FAMILY MEMBER
- ◻ SPEND TIME OUTDOORS
- ◻ HAVE A MINI PAMPER SESSION
- ◻ CUDDLE A PET
- ◻ TRY SOMETHING NEW
- ◻ READ A BOOK

Make it a habit to take care of yourself!

THIS WEEK
I AM GRATEFUL FOR

Monthly PLANNER

SUN	MON	TUE	WED

JUL   OCT

AUG   NOV

SEP   DEC   YEAR ____________

<u>Worship Song of the Month</u>
"Nobody Greater"
by Vashawn Mitchell

THU	FRI	SAT	NOTES

Quarterly Accountability

What do you want to accomplish over this quarter?

What did you actually accomplish?

"I am a valuable person."

"I accept things for what they are."

____

____

____

____

____

____

____

DAILY GOALS

☐

☐

☐

DAILY TASKS

☐

☐

☐

"*I am in competition with no one.*"

"I am favored."

DAILY GOALS

DAILY TASKS

____

"I am humble."

____

____

____

____

____

____

____

____

DAILY GOALS

_______________________________ ☐

_______________________________ ☐

_______________________________ ☐

DAILY TASKS

_______________________________ ☐

_______________________________ ☐

_______________________________ ☐

"I am content with being in my own company."

DAILY GOALS

DAILY TASKS

"I do not seek revenge."

Self-Care Saturday

- ☐ EAT THREE MAIN MEALS
- ☐ GO ON A 24-HOUR SOCIAL MEDIA DETOX
- ☐ FIND A QUIET SPOT TO MEDITATE
- ☐ LIGHT AN AROMATIC CANDLE
- ☐ DO A GRATITUDE LIST
- ☐ PRACTICE DEEP BREATHING
- ☐ LISTEN TO GOOD MUSIC
- ☐ EXERCISE
- ☐ CATCH UP WITH A FRIEND
- ☐ VISIT A FAMILY MEMBER
- ☐ SPEND TIME OUTDOORS
- ☐ HAVE A MINI PAMPER SESSION
- ☐ CUDDLE A PET
- ☐ TRY SOMETHING NEW
- ☐ READ A BOOK

Make it a habit to take care of yourself!

THIS WEEK
I AM GRATEFUL FOR

"I am not an 'attention seeker'."

DAILY GOALS

DAILY TASKS

"I utilize my time wisely."

"I am mature in my prayer life."

DAILY GOALS

DAILY TASKS

"I am the reason someone believes in good people."

DAILY GOALS

DAILY TASKS

"I do not judge people, knowingly and unknowingly."

"_I am giving._"

DAILY GOALS

○
○
○

DAILY TASKS

○
○
○

"I am appreciative of every season I am in."

____

____

____

____

____

____

____

DAILY GOALS

_________________________________ ○
_________________________________ ○
_________________________________ ○

DAILY TASKS

_________________________________ ○
_________________________________ ○
_________________________________ ○

Self-Care Saturday

CHECK THE BOXES OF THE ACTIVITIES YOU DO TO TAKE CARE OF YOURSELF.

- ☐ EAT THREE MAIN MEALS
- ☐ GO ON A 24-HOUR SOCIAL MEDIA DETOX
- ☐ FIND A QUIET SPOT TO MEDITATE
- ☐ LIGHT AN AROMATIC CANDLE
- ☐ DO A GRATITUDE LIST
- ☐ PRACTICE DEEP BREATHING
- ☐ LISTEN TO GOOD MUSIC
- ☐ EXERCISE
- ☐ CATCH UP WITH A FRIEND
- ☐ VISIT A FAMILY MEMBER
- ☐ SPEND TIME OUTDOORS
- ☐ HAVE A MINI PAMPER SESSION
- ☐ CUDDLE A PET
- ☐ TRY SOMETHING NEW
- ☐ READ A BOOK

Make it a habit to take care of yourself!

THIS WEEK

I AM GRATEFUL FOR

DAILY GOALS

DAILY TASKS

"I do not compare myself to others."

"I love the person I am becoming more and more each day."

"I am content with if it happens or if it does not."

DAILY GOALS

DAILY TASKS

"I do not take things personally."

DAILY GOALS

○
○
○

DAILY TASKS

○
○
○

"I celebrate my wins and losses."

DAILY GOALS

DAILY TASKS

"*I am supportive.*"

Self-Care Saturday

CHECK THE BOXES OF THE ACTIVITIES YOU DO TO TAKE CARE OF YOURSELF.

- EAT THREE MAIN MEALS
- GO ON A 24-HOUR SOCIAL MEDIA DETOX
- FIND A QUIET SPOT TO MEDITATE
- LIGHT AN AROMATIC CANDLE
- DO A GRATITUDE LIST
- PRACTICE DEEP BREATHING
- LISTEN TO GOOD MUSIC
- EXERCISE
- CATCH UP WITH A FRIEND
- VISIT A FAMILY MEMBER
- SPEND TIME OUTDOORS
- HAVE A MINI PAMPER SESSION
- CUDDLE A PET
- TRY SOMETHING NEW
- READ A BOOK

Make it a habit to take care of yourself!

THIS WEEK
I AM GRATEFUL FOR

DAILY GOALS

DAILY TASKS

> # "I do not envy other people."

"I am the same person 24 hours a day, 7 days a week."

DAILY GOALS

DAILY TASKS

"I express love more as a verb (action) than a noun (descriptive word)."

DAILY GOALS

DAILY TASKS

"*Being thankful is not a seasonal thing.*"

"*My priorities are in order.*"

> *"I control my anxiety,
> not vice versa."*

Self-Care Saturday

CHECK THE BOXES OF THE ACTIVITIES YOU DO TO TAKE CARE OF YOURSELF.

- ☐ EAT THREE MAIN MEALS
- ☐ GO ON A 24-HOUR SOCIAL MEDIA DETOX
- ☐ FIND A QUIET SPOT TO MEDITATE
- ☐ LIGHT AN AROMATIC CANDLE
- ☐ DO A GRATITUDE LIST
- ☐ PRACTICE DEEP BREATHING
- ☐ LISTEN TO GOOD MUSIC
- ☐ EXERCISE
- ☐ CATCH UP WITH A FRIEND
- ☐ VISIT A FAMILY MEMBER
- ☐ SPEND TIME OUTDOORS
- ☐ HAVE A MINI PAMPER SESSION
- ☐ CUDDLE A PET
- ☐ TRY SOMETHING NEW
- ☐ READ A BOOK

Make it a habit to take care of yourself!

THIS WEEK
I AM GRATEFUL FOR

"Forgiveness does not require reconnection."

DAILY GOALS

DAILY TASKS

"*I do not make assumptions.*"

"I am content with being right AND wrong."

Monthly PLANNER

JAN
FEB
MAR

APR
MAY
JUN

SUN	MON	TUE	WED

JUL	OCT		
AUG	NOV		
SEP	DEC	YEAR ____________	

THU	FRI	SAT	NOTES

"I learn from my mistakes."

"I do not make excuses."

"There is more to me than my physical attributes."

DAILY GOALS

○
○
○

DAILY TASKS

○
○
○

"I have integrity."

DAILY GOALS

DAILY TASKS

"I do not sweat the 'small stuff'."

DAILY GOALS

DAILY TASKS

"I am fearless."

"Giving up is never an option."

Self-Care Saturday

CHECK THE BOXES OF THE ACTIVITIES YOU DO TO TAKE CARE OF YOURSELF.

- ☐ EAT THREE MAIN MEALS
- ☐ GO ON A 24-HOUR SOCIAL MEDIA DETOX
- ☐ FIND A QUIET SPOT TO MEDITATE
- ☐ LIGHT AN AROMATIC CANDLE
- ☐ DO A GRATITUDE LIST
- ☐ PRACTICE DEEP BREATHING
- ☐ LISTEN TO GOOD MUSIC
- ☐ EXERCISE
- ☐ CATCH UP WITH A FRIEND
- ☐ VISIT A FAMILY MEMBER
- ☐ SPEND TIME OUTDOORS
- ☐ HAVE A MINI PAMPER SESSION
- ☐ CUDDLE A PET
- ☐ TRY SOMETHING NEW
- ☐ READ A BOOK

Make it a habit to take care of yourself!

THIS WEEK

I AM GRATEFUL FOR

"I do not put off until tomorrow what I can do today."

DAILY GOALS

DAILY TASKS

"I choose happiness in this moment over the pain of my past."

____

____

____

____

____

____

____

DAILY GOALS

○

○

○

DAILY TASKS

○

○

○

> *"My past does not define who I am today."*

"God has the final say, not man."

"I ask for God's approval before making decisions."

DAILY GOALS

DAILY TASKS

"There is a bright future ahead of me."

DAILY GOALS

DAILY TASKS

"I am the head and not the tail. I am above and not beneath." - Deuteronomy 28:13

Self-Care Saturday

CHECK THE BOXES OF THE ACTIVITIES YOU DO TO TAKE CARE OF YOURSELF.

- ☐ EAT THREE MAIN MEALS
- ☐ GO ON A 24-HOUR SOCIAL MEDIA DETOX
- ☐ FIND A QUIET SPOT TO MEDITATE
- ☐ LIGHT AN AROMATIC CANDLE
- ☐ DO A GRATITUDE LIST
- ☐ PRACTICE DEEP BREATHING
- ☐ LISTEN TO GOOD MUSIC
- ☐ EXERCISE
- ☐ CATCH UP WITH A FRIEND
- ☐ VISIT A FAMILY MEMBER
- ☐ SPEND TIME OUTDOORS
- ☐ HAVE A MINI PAMPER SESSION
- ☐ CUDDLE A PET
- ☐ TRY SOMETHING NEW
- ☐ READ A BOOK

Make it a habit to take care of yourself!

THIS WEEK

I AM GRATEFUL FOR

____

____

____

____

____

____

____

DAILY GOALS

○
○
○

DAILY TASKS

○
○
○

"I express self love everyday."

____

____

____

____

____

____

____

DAILY GOALS

_______________________________ ◯
_______________________________ ◯
_______________________________ ◯

DAILY TASKS

_______________________________ ◻
_______________________________ ◻
_______________________________ ◻

"I have a great relationship with the people in my life."

DAILY GOALS

DAILY TASKS

"My intimate relationship with God becomes stronger each day."

"I am driven."

DAILY GOALS

DAILY TASKS

"I apologize when I am wrong."

DAILY GOALS

DAILY TASKS

Self-Care Saturday

- [ ] EAT THREE MAIN MEALS
- [ ] GO ON A 24-HOUR SOCIAL MEDIA DETOX
- [ ] FIND A QUIET SPOT TO MEDITATE
- [ ] LIGHT AN AROMATIC CANDLE
- [ ] DO A GRATITUDE LIST
- [ ] PRACTICE DEEP BREATHING
- [ ] LISTEN TO GOOD MUSIC
- [ ] EXERCISE
- [ ] CATCH UP WITH A FRIEND
- [ ] VISIT A FAMILY MEMBER
- [ ] SPEND TIME OUTDOORS
- [ ] HAVE A MINI PAMPER SESSION
- [ ] CUDDLE A PET
- [ ] TRY SOMETHING NEW
- [ ] READ A BOOK

Make it a habit to take care of yourself!

THIS WEEK

I AM GRATEFUL FOR

"I am gentle with myself."

DAILY GOALS

DAILY TASKS

"I am content with not knowing something because I do not know everything."

"I am trustworthy."

"I am responsible."

____

"I am loyal."

____

____

____

____

____

____

____

____

DAILY GOALS

____________________________ ⬭

____________________________ ⬭

____________________________ ⬭

DAILY TASKS

____________________________ ⬭

____________________________ ⬭

____________________________ ⬭

"*I am an organized person.*"

DAILY GOALS

DAILY TASKS

"I have been broken to be built."

Self-Care
Saturday

CHECK THE BOXES OF THE ACTIVITIES YOU DO TO TAKE CARE OF YOURSELF.

- ☐ EAT THREE MAIN MEALS
- ☐ GO ON A 24-HOUR SOCIAL MEDIA DETOX
- ☐ FIND A QUIET SPOT TO MEDITATE
- ☐ LIGHT AN AROMATIC CANDLE
- ☐ DO A GRATITUDE LIST
- ☐ PRACTICE DEEP BREATHING
- ☐ LISTEN TO GOOD MUSIC
- ☐ EXERCISE
- ☐ CATCH UP WITH A FRIEND
- ☐ VISIT A FAMILY MEMBER
- ☐ SPEND TIME OUTDOORS
- ☐ HAVE A MINI PAMPER SESSION
- ☐ CUDDLE A PET
- ☐ TRY SOMETHING NEW
- ☐ READ A BOOK

Make it a habit to take care of yourself!

THIS WEEK

I AM GRATEFUL FOR

"I do right by everyone."

DAILY GOALS

DAILY TASKS

"I embrace the
compliments I receive."

DAILY GOALS

DAILY TASKS

SUN	MON	TUE	WED

JUL   OCT

AUG   NOV

SEP   DEC   YEAR ________________

THU	FRI	SAT	NOTES

"I protect my energy."

DAILY GOALS

○
○
○

DAILY TASKS

○
○
○

"I preserve my peace."

"I believe in myself."

DAILY GOALS

○
○
○

DAILY TASKS

○
○
○

"I set realistic goals."

DAILY GOALS

DAILY TASKS

"I am consistent."

"I am very descriptive when I pray."

"My time is too precious to waste."

Self-Care Saturday

THIS WEEK

I AM GRATEFUL FOR

> # "I do not act like I am better than anyone."

DAILY GOALS

- ○
- ○ ○
- ○ ○

DAILY TASKS

- ○
- ○ ○
- ○ ○

"*I speak eloquently.*"

DAILY GOALS

DAILY TASKS

"Today is going to be
an amazing day."

"I am a blessing to others."

DAILY GOALS

DAILY TASKS

DAILY GOALS

DAILY TASKS

DAILY GOALS

DAILY TASKS

"It is not always about me."

DAILY GOALS

DAILY TASKS

Self-Care Saturday

CHECK THE BOXES OF THE ACTIVITIES YOU DO TO TAKE CARE OF YOURSELF.

- ☐ EAT THREE MAIN MEALS
- ☐ GO ON A 24-HOUR SOCIAL MEDIA DETOX
- ☐ FIND A QUIET SPOT TO MEDITATE
- ☐ LIGHT AN AROMATIC CANDLE
- ☐ DO A GRATITUDE LIST
- ☐ PRACTICE DEEP BREATHING
- ☐ LISTEN TO GOOD MUSIC
- ☐ EXERCISE
- ☐ CATCH UP WITH A FRIEND
- ☐ VISIT A FAMILY MEMBER
- ☐ SPEND TIME OUTDOORS
- ☐ HAVE A MINI PAMPER SESSION
- ☐ CUDDLE A PET
- ☐ TRY SOMETHING NEW
- ☐ READ A BOOK

Make it a habit to take care of yourself!

THIS WEEK

I AM GRATEFUL FOR

"I am disciplined."

> "God speaks to me
> and through me."

"I am honest with myself."

DAILY GOALS

○
○
○

DAILY TASKS

○
○
○

"I do not ignore the red flags."

"I work well under pressure."

DAILY GOALS

DAILY TASKS

"I am filled with laughter."

DAILY GOALS

DAILY TASKS

DAILY GOALS

DAILY TASKS

Self-Care Saturday

CHECK THE BOXES OF THE ACTIVITIES YOU DO TO TAKE CARE OF YOURSELF.

- ⬜ EAT THREE MAIN MEALS
- ⬜ GO ON A 24-HOUR SOCIAL MEDIA DETOX
- ⬜ FIND A QUIET SPOT TO MEDITATE
- ⬜ LIGHT AN AROMATIC CANDLE
- ⬜ DO A GRATITUDE LIST
- ⬜ PRACTICE DEEP BREATHING
- ⬜ LISTEN TO GOOD MUSIC
- ⬜ EXERCISE
- ⬜ CATCH UP WITH A FRIEND
- ⬜ VISIT A FAMILY MEMBER
- ⬜ SPEND TIME OUTDOORS
- ⬜ HAVE A MINI PAMPER SESSION
- ⬜ CUDDLE A PET
- ⬜ TRY SOMETHING NEW
- ⬜ READ A BOOK

Make it a habit to take care of yourself!

THIS WEEK

I AM GRATEFUL FOR

"For [God] knows the plans He has for [me]." -Jeremiah 29:11

DAILY GOALS

DAILY TASKS

"I have faith the size of a mustard seed."
-Matthew 17:20

DAILY GOALS

DAILY TASKS

DAILY GOALS

DAILY TASKS

"I wholeheartedly want what God wants for my life."

DAILY GOALS

DAILY TASKS

"God is always with me."

"I am full of wisdom."

"I have patience."

____

____

____

____

____

____

____

DAILY GOALS

____ ◯

____ ◯

____ ◯

DAILY TASKS

____ ◯

____ ◯

____ ◯

Self-Care Saturday

CHECK THE BOXES OF THE ACTIVITIES YOU DO TO TAKE CARE OF YOURSELF.

- ☐ EAT THREE MAIN MEALS
- ☐ GO ON A 24-HOUR SOCIAL MEDIA DETOX
- ☐ FIND A QUIET SPOT TO MEDITATE
- ☐ LIGHT AN AROMATIC CANDLE
- ☐ DO A GRATITUDE LIST
- ☐ PRACTICE DEEP BREATHING
- ☐ LISTEN TO GOOD MUSIC
- ☐ EXERCISE
- ☐ CATCH UP WITH A FRIEND
- ☐ VISIT A FAMILY MEMBER
- ☐ SPEND TIME OUTDOORS
- ☐ HAVE A MINI PAMPER SESSION
- ☐ CUDDLE A PET
- ☐ TRY SOMETHING NEW
- ☐ READ A BOOK

Make it a habit to take care of yourself!

THIS WEEK
I AM GRATEFUL FOR

"I am restored."

"The dead things in my life have been revived."

DAILY GOALS

DAILY TASKS

"I trust in God's timing."

____

____

____

____

____

____

____

DAILY GOALS

____ ○
____ ○
____ ○

DAILY TASKS

____ ▢
____ ▢
____ ▢

"Don't compare your life to others. There's no comparison between the sun and the moon. They shine when it's their time."
-Anonymous

Monthly PLANNER

JAN
FEB
MAR

APR
MAY
JUN

SUN	MON	TUE	WED

JUL OCT

AUG NOV

SEP DEC YEAR _________________

THU	FRI	SAT	NOTES

Quarterly Accountability

What do you want to accomplish over this quarter?

What did you actually accomplish?

"I am talented."

"There is no better time than now."

> "I treat people the way
> I want to be treated."

"God validates who I am."

"I think outside of the box."

DAILY GOALS

DAILY TASKS

____

"God is the center of my life."

____

____

____

____

____

____

____

____

DAILY GOALS

_______________________________________ ○

_______________________________________ ○

_______________________________________ ○

DAILY TASKS

_______________________________________ ○

_______________________________________ ○

_______________________________________ ○

"I am "quick to listen, slow to speak, and slow to get angry." -James 1:19

____

____

____

____

____

____

____

CHECK THE BOXES OF THE ACTIVITIES YOU DO TO TAKE CARE OF YOURSELF.

- ☐ EAT THREE MAIN MEALS
- ☐ GO ON A 24-HOUR SOCIAL MEDIA DETOX
- ☐ FIND A QUIET SPOT TO MEDITATE
- ☐ LIGHT AN AROMATIC CANDLE
- ☐ DO A GRATITUDE LIST
- ☐ PRACTICE DEEP BREATHING
- ☐ LISTEN TO GOOD MUSIC
- ☐ EXERCISE
- ☐ CATCH UP WITH A FRIEND
- ☐ VISIT A FAMILY MEMBER
- ☐ SPEND TIME OUTDOORS
- ☐ HAVE A MINI PAMPER SESSION
- ☐ CUDDLE A PET
- ☐ TRY SOMETHING NEW
- ☐ READ A BOOK

Make it a habit to take care of yourself!

THIS WEEK

I AM GRATEFUL FOR

____

"Keep striving, for God gives his hardest battles to His strongest soliders." -Habeeb Akande

____

____

____

____

____

____

____

DAILY GOALS

________________________________ ◯

________________________________ ◯

________________________________ ◯

DAILY TASKS

________________________________ ◯

________________________________ ◯

________________________________ ◯

> *"I find joy in the smallest things."*

DAILY GOALS

DAILY TASKS

DAILY GOALS

DAILY TASKS

"I choose faith over fear."

____

"I live my life to the fullest."

____

"I uplift people."

____

____

____

____

____

____

____

____

DAILY GOALS

____ ○

____ ○

____ ○

DAILY TASKS

____ ○

____ ○

____ ○

"I am vibrant."

DAILY GOALS

DAILY TASKS

Self-Care Saturday

CHECK THE BOXES OF THE ACTIVITIES YOU DO TO TAKE CARE OF YOURSELF.

- ◯ EAT THREE MAIN MEALS
- ◯ GO ON A 24-HOUR SOCIAL MEDIA DETOX
- ◯ FIND A QUIET SPOT TO MEDITATE
- ◯ LIGHT AN AROMATIC CANDLE
- ◯ DO A GRATITUDE LIST
- ◯ PRACTICE DEEP BREATHING
- ◯ LISTEN TO GOOD MUSIC
- ◯ EXERCISE
- ◯ CATCH UP WITH A FRIEND
- ◯ VISIT A FAMILY MEMBER
- ◯ SPEND TIME OUTDOORS
- ◯ HAVE A MINI PAMPER SESSION
- ◯ CUDDLE A PET
- ◯ TRY SOMETHING NEW
- ◯ READ A BOOK

Make it a habit to take care of yourself!

THIS WEEK
I AM GRATEFUL FOR

"I am amazing."

____

____

____

____

____

____

____

DAILY GOALS

_______________ ◯

_______________ ◯

_______________ ◯

DAILY TASKS

_______________ ◯

_______________ ◯

_______________ ◯

"I am passionate."

"I am successful."

"I am optimistic."

DAILY GOALS

DAILY TASKS

"I am a positive person."

____

____

____

____

____

____

____

DAILY GOALS

_______________________________________ ○

_______________________________________ ○

_______________________________________ ○

DAILY TASKS

_______________________________________ ○

_______________________________________ ○

_______________________________________ ○

"I do not overlook the simple things."

DAILY GOALS

DAILY TASKS

"I may not be where I want, but I am not where I used to be."

Self-Care Saturday

CHECK THE BOXES OF THE ACTIVITIES YOU DO TO TAKE CARE OF YOURSELF.

- [ ] EAT THREE MAIN MEALS
- [ ] GO ON A 24-HOUR SOCIAL MEDIA DETOX
- [ ] FIND A QUIET SPOT TO MEDITATE
- [ ] LIGHT AN AROMATIC CANDLE
- [ ] DO A GRATITUDE LIST
- [ ] PRACTICE DEEP BREATHING
- [ ] LISTEN TO GOOD MUSIC
- [ ] EXERCISE
- [ ] CATCH UP WITH A FRIEND
- [ ] VISIT A FAMILY MEMBER
- [ ] SPEND TIME OUTDOORS
- [ ] HAVE A MINI PAMPER SESSION
- [ ] CUDDLE A PET
- [ ] TRY SOMETHING NEW
- [ ] READ A BOOK

Make it a habit to take care of yourself!

THIS WEEK
I AM GRATEFUL FOR

"I am genuine."

"I have a good heart posture."

"*I am a time-oriented person.*"

DAILY GOALS

DAILY TASKS

"I show some sort
of gratitude daily."

DAILY GOALS

DAILY TASKS

"What God has for me cannot be taken by anyone else."

"I know my identity."

"I say what I mean and mean what I say."

Self-Care Saturday

CHECK THE BOXES OF THE ACTIVITIES YOU DO TO TAKE CARE OF YOURSELF.

- ☐ EAT THREE MAIN MEALS
- ☐ GO ON A 24-HOUR SOCIAL MEDIA DETOX
- ☐ FIND A QUIET SPOT TO MEDITATE
- ☐ LIGHT AN AROMATIC CANDLE
- ☐ DO A GRATITUDE LIST
- ☐ PRACTICE DEEP BREATHING
- ☐ LISTEN TO GOOD MUSIC
- ☐ EXERCISE
- ☐ CATCH UP WITH A FRIEND
- ☐ VISIT A FAMILY MEMBER
- ☐ SPEND TIME OUTDOORS
- ☐ HAVE A MINI PAMPER SESSION
- ☐ CUDDLE A PET
- ☐ TRY SOMETHING NEW
- ☐ READ A BOOK

Make it a habit to take care of yourself!

THIS WEEK

I AM GRATEFUL FOR

"I do not contradict myself."

"I follow in my own shadow."

Have you said your daily affirmation(s) for the day? If you answered 'no' it's not too late!

Monthly PLANNER

SUN	MON	TUE	WED

JUL

AUG

SEP

OCT

NOV

DEC

YEAR _______________

<u>Worship Song of the Month</u>
"Lord You Are Good"
by Todd Galberth

THU	FRI	SAT	NOTES

"God is always in control."

DAILY TASKS

"Some things are better left unsaid."

____

"I am focused."

____

____

____

____

____

____

____

____

____

"I embrace my imperfections."

____

____

____

____

____

____

____

____

DAILY GOALS

_______________________________________ ○
_______________________________________ ○
_______________________________________ ○

DAILY TASKS

_______________________________________ ○
_______________________________________ ○
_______________________________________ ○

DAILY GOALS

DAILY TASKS

"I love my life!"

DAILY GOALS

DAILY TASKS

"I stand out from others."

DAILY GOALS

DAILY TASKS

Self-Care Saturday

CHECK THE BOXES OF THE ACTIVITIES YOU DO TO TAKE CARE OF YOURSELF.

- ☐ EAT THREE MAIN MEALS
- ☐ GO ON A 24-HOUR SOCIAL MEDIA DETOX
- ☐ FIND A QUIET SPOT TO MEDITATE
- ☐ LIGHT AN AROMATIC CANDLE
- ☐ DO A GRATITUDE LIST
- ☐ PRACTICE DEEP BREATHING
- ☐ LISTEN TO GOOD MUSIC
- ☐ EXERCISE
- ☐ CATCH UP WITH A FRIEND
- ☐ VISIT A FAMILY MEMBER
- ☐ SPEND TIME OUTDOORS
- ☐ HAVE A MINI PAMPER SESSION
- ☐ CUDDLE A PET
- ☐ TRY SOMETHING NEW
- ☐ READ A BOOK

Make it a habit to take care of yourself!

THIS WEEK

I AM GRATEFUL FOR

____

____

____

____

____

____

____

DAILY GOALS

_______________________________________ ⭕

_______________________________________ ⭕

_______________________________________ ⭕

DAILY TASKS

_______________________________________ ⭕

_______________________________________ ⭕

_______________________________________ ⭕

"I show grace to others."

"I lead by example."

"*My life reflects my values.*"

"I am getting rid of bad habits."

"I have an intimate relationship with God."

> *"I do not forget about God when I get what I prayed for."*

DAILY GOALS

DAILY TASKS

Self-Care Saturday

CHECK THE BOXES OF THE ACTIVITIES YOU DO TO TAKE CARE OF YOURSELF.

- ☐ EAT THREE MAIN MEALS
- ☐ GO ON A 24-HOUR SOCIAL MEDIA DETOX
- ☐ FIND A QUIET SPOT TO MEDITATE
- ☐ LIGHT AN AROMATIC CANDLE
- ☐ DO A GRATITUDE LIST
- ☐ PRACTICE DEEP BREATHING
- ☐ LISTEN TO GOOD MUSIC
- ☐ EXERCISE
- ☐ CATCH UP WITH A FRIEND
- ☐ VISIT A FAMILY MEMBER
- ☐ SPEND TIME OUTDOORS
- ☐ HAVE A MINI PAMPER SESSION
- ☐ CUDDLE A PET
- ☐ TRY SOMETHING NEW
- ☐ READ A BOOK

Make it a habit to take care of yourself!

THIS WEEK

I AM GRATEFUL FOR

"Because I still have a pulse, I still have a purpose."

___

DAILY GOALS

DAILY TASKS

"I am enough."

DAILY GOALS

DAILY TASKS

"God always makes a way."

DAILY GOALS

DAILY TASKS

"*I stand up for myself.*"

DAILY GOALS

DAILY TASKS

"I mind my own business."

"I celebrate the unknown and the unseen."

Self-Care Saturday

CHECK THE BOXES OF THE ACTIVITIES YOU DO TO TAKE CARE OF YOURSELF.

- ○ EAT THREE MAIN MEALS
- ○ GO ON A 24-HOUR SOCIAL MEDIA DETOX
- ○ FIND A QUIET SPOT TO MEDITATE
- ○ LIGHT AN AROMATIC CANDLE
- ○ DO A GRATITUDE LIST
- ○ PRACTICE DEEP BREATHING
- ○ LISTEN TO GOOD MUSIC
- ○ EXERCISE
- ○ CATCH UP WITH A FRIEND
- ○ VISIT A FAMILY MEMBER
- ○ SPEND TIME OUTDOORS
- ○ HAVE A MINI PAMPER SESSION
- ○ CUDDLE A PET
- ○ TRY SOMETHING NEW
- ○ READ A BOOK

Make it a habit to take care of yourself!

THIS WEEK
I AM GRATEFUL FOR

"I am determined."

DAILY GOALS

DAILY TASKS

> "I am thankful for the love I receive
> and I extend that same love."

DAILY GOALS

○
○
○

DAILY TASKS

○
○
○

"I strive to do better."

"I am happy to be
alive and well."

DAILY GOALS

DAILY TASKS

DAILY GOALS

DAILY TASKS

"I am ready to receive love."

DAILY GOALS

DAILY TASKS

Self-Care Saturday

CHECK THE BOXES OF THE ACTIVITIES YOU DO TO TAKE CARE OF YOURSELF.

- ☐ EAT THREE MAIN MEALS
- ☐ GO ON A 24-HOUR SOCIAL MEDIA DETOX
- ☐ FIND A QUIET SPOT TO MEDITATE
- ☐ LIGHT AN AROMATIC CANDLE
- ☐ DO A GRATITUDE LIST
- ☐ PRACTICE DEEP BREATHING
- ☐ LISTEN TO GOOD MUSIC
- ☐ EXERCISE
- ☐ CATCH UP WITH A FRIEND
- ☐ VISIT A FAMILY MEMBER
- ☐ SPEND TIME OUTDOORS
- ☐ HAVE A MINI PAMPER SESSION
- ☐ CUDDLE A PET
- ☐ TRY SOMETHING NEW
- ☐ READ A BOOK

Make it a habit to take care of yourself!

THIS WEEK

I AM GRATEFUL FOR

"I set aside time for God everyday."

DAILY GOALS

DAILY TASKS

"I fix my eyes on God."

"I am grateful for the support I have in my life."

DAILY GOALS

DAILY TASKS

Genesis 1:27 (NLT)–"So God created human beings in his own image. In the name of God he created them; male and female he created them."

Monthly PLANNER

JAN FEB MAR APR MAY JUN

SUN	MON	TUE	WED

Worship Song of the Month
"Worth"
by Anthony Brown

THU	FRI	SAT	NOTES

"I am caring."

DAILY GOALS

DAILY TASKS

"I know the true value of a moment before it becomes a memory."

DAILY GOALS

DAILY TASKS

____

"I cherish memories."

____

____

____

____

____

____

____

____

DAILY GOALS

DAILY TASKS

"My present situation is not my final destination."

"The best is yet to come."

"I give my problems to God because they are out of my control."

DAILY GOALS

DAILY TASKS

"God knows my heart."

DAILY GOALS

DAILY TASKS

Self-Care Saturday

CHECK THE BOXES OF THE ACTIVITIES YOU DO TO TAKE CARE OF YOURSELF.

- EAT THREE MAIN MEALS
- GO ON A 24-HOUR SOCIAL MEDIA DETOX
- FIND A QUIET SPOT TO MEDITATE
- LIGHT AN AROMATIC CANDLE
- DO A GRATITUDE LIST
- PRACTICE DEEP BREATHING
- LISTEN TO GOOD MUSIC
- EXERCISE
- CATCH UP WITH A FRIEND
- VISIT A FAMILY MEMBER
- SPEND TIME OUTDOORS
- HAVE A MINI PAMPER SESSION
- CUDDLE A PET
- TRY SOMETHING NEW
- READ A BOOK

Make it a habit to take care of yourself!

THIS WEEK

I AM GRATEFUL FOR

"I let go of things I cannot control."

DAILY GOALS

○
○
○

DAILY TASKS

○
○
○

"I am an inspiration to others."

____

____

____

____

____

____

____

DAILY GOALS

○
○
○

DAILY TASKS

○
○
○

"*I do not invest too much emotion into one thing.*"

DAILY GOALS

DAILY TASKS

"[I] am never too old to set another goal
or to dream a new dream." -C.S. Lewis

DAILY GOALS

DAILY TASKS

"I do not take anyone or anything for granted."

DAILY GOALS

DAILY TASKS

Self-Care Saturday

CHECK THE BOXES OF THE ACTIVITIES YOU DO TO TAKE CARE OF YOURSELF.

- ⃝ EAT THREE MAIN MEALS
- ⃝ GO ON A 24-HOUR SOCIAL MEDIA DETOX
- ⃝ FIND A QUIET SPOT TO MEDITATE
- ⃝ LIGHT AN AROMATIC CANDLE
- ⃝ DO A GRATITUDE LIST
- ⃝ PRACTICE DEEP BREATHING
- ⃝ LISTEN TO GOOD MUSIC
- ⃝ EXERCISE
- ⃝ CATCH UP WITH A FRIEND
- ⃝ VISIT A FAMILY MEMBER
- ⃝ SPEND TIME OUTDOORS
- ⃝ HAVE A MINI PAMPER SESSION
- ⃝ CUDDLE A PET
- ⃝ TRY SOMETHING NEW
- ⃝ READ A BOOK

Make it a habit to take care of yourself!

THIS WEEK
I AM GRATEFUL FOR

"I have inner peace."

DAILY GOALS

DAILY TASKS

"I have made peace with my past."

DAILY GOALS

DAILY TASKS

"I am the only person in charge of my happiness."

“*I do not dwell on the past.*”

"Time heals almost everything,
so I give things time."

____

____

____

____

____

____

____

DAILY GOALS

○
○
○

DAILY TASKS

○
○
○

DAILY GOALS

DAILY TASKS

"I see the good in myself."

Self-Care Saturday

CHECK THE BOXES OF THE ACTIVITIES YOU DO TO TAKE CARE OF YOURSELF.

- EAT THREE MAIN MEALS
- GO ON A 24-HOUR SOCIAL MEDIA DETOX
- FIND A QUIET SPOT TO MEDITATE
- LIGHT AN AROMATIC CANDLE
- DO A GRATITUDE LIST
- PRACTICE DEEP BREATHING
- LISTEN TO GOOD MUSIC
- EXERCISE
- CATCH UP WITH A FRIEND
- VISIT A FAMILY MEMBER
- SPEND TIME OUTDOORS
- HAVE A MINI PAMPER SESSION
- CUDDLE A PET
- TRY SOMETHING NEW
- READ A BOOK

Make it a habit to take care of yourself!

THIS WEEK
I AM GRATEFUL FOR

"I do not replay
failed scenarios."

DAILY GOALS

DAILY TASKS

DAILY GOALS

DAILY TASKS

"I think before I act or speak."

DAILY GOALS

DAILY TASKS

"Unlearning things that were taught by people who did not know what they were doing themselves, is ok."

DAILY GOALS

DAILY TASKS

"Growing is uncomfortable and
I am content with that."

"I do what feels uncomfortable."

____

____

____

____

____

____

____

DAILY GOALS

_______________________________________ ○

_______________________________________ ○

_______________________________________ ○

DAILY TASKS

_______________________________________ ○

_______________________________________ ○

_______________________________________ ○

"I am created in God's image."

Self-Care Saturday

CHECK THE BOXES OF THE ACTIVITIES YOU DO TO TAKE CARE OF YOURSELF.

- ☐ EAT THREE MAIN MEALS
- ☐ GO ON A 24-HOUR SOCIAL MEDIA DETOX
- ☐ FIND A QUIET SPOT TO MEDITATE
- ☐ LIGHT AN AROMATIC CANDLE
- ☐ DO A GRATITUDE LIST
- ☐ PRACTICE DEEP BREATHING
- ☐ LISTEN TO GOOD MUSIC
- ☐ EXERCISE
- ☐ CATCH UP WITH A FRIEND
- ☐ VISIT A FAMILY MEMBER
- ☐ SPEND TIME OUTDOORS
- ☐ HAVE A MINI PAMPER SESSION
- ☐ CUDDLE A PET
- ☐ TRY SOMETHING NEW
- ☐ READ A BOOK

Make it a habit to take care of yourself!

THIS WEEK

I AM GRATEFUL FOR

> ## "I let go of the need to explain or justify my behavior."

____

____

____

____

____

____

____

DAILY GOALS

- ○
- ○
- ○

DAILY TASKS

- ○
- ○
- ○

"I let go of the need for others' approval or agreement."

<hr>

"I adjust well to change."

<hr>

"Where there is no accountability there will also be no responsibility." -Sunday Adelaja

JAN
FEB
MAR
APR
MAY
JUN

Monthly PLANNER

SUN

MON

TUE

WED

JUL   OCT

AUG   NOV

SEP   DEC   YEAR ___________________

THU	FRI	SAT	NOTES

Quarterly Accountability

What do you want to accomplish over this quarter?

What did you actually accomplish?

"I am not distracted by anything that is associated with my goals."

"I give up the illusion that I deserve
a problem-free life."

DAILY GOALS

DAILY TASKS

"*The past cannot be changed.*"

"Everyone's journey is different."

DAILY GOALS

DAILY TASKS

"Positive thoughts create positive things."

DAILY GOALS

DAILY TASKS

"Being kind to someone does not cost me a thing."

DAILY GOALS

DAILY TASKS

____

____

____

____

____

____

DAILY GOALS

____ ○

____ ○

____ ○

DAILY TASKS

____ ○

____ ○

____ ○

Self-Care Saturday

CHECK THE BOXES OF THE ACTIVITIES YOU DO TO TAKE CARE OF YOURSELF.

- ⬜ EAT THREE MAIN MEALS
- ⬜ GO ON A 24-HOUR SOCIAL MEDIA DETOX
- ⬜ FIND A QUIET SPOT TO MEDITATE
- ⬜ LIGHT AN AROMATIC CANDLE
- ⬜ DO A GRATITUDE LIST
- ⬜ PRACTICE DEEP BREATHING
- ⬜ LISTEN TO GOOD MUSIC
- ⬜ EXERCISE
- ⬜ CATCH UP WITH A FRIEND
- ⬜ VISIT A FAMILY MEMBER
- ⬜ SPEND TIME OUTDOORS
- ⬜ HAVE A MINI PAMPER SESSION
- ⬜ CUDDLE A PET
- ⬜ TRY SOMETHING NEW
- ⬜ READ A BOOK

Make it a habit to take care of yourself!

"Healing is not an overnight process."

"I do not get discouraged."

DAILY GOALS

DAILY TASKS

"I take each day one step at a time."

DAILY GOALS

○ ○ ○

DAILY TASKS

○ ○ ○

____

"Challenges are what make life interesting and overcoming them is what makes life meaningful." -Joshua J. Marine

____

____

____

____

____

____

____

____

DAILY GOALS

_______________________________________ ○
_______________________________________ ○
_______________________________________ ○

DAILY TASKS

_______________________________________ ○
_______________________________________ ○
_______________________________________ ○

"I live without the fear of making mistakes."

"Be a better you, for you."
-Sonya Teclai

____

____

____

____

____

____

____

DAILY GOALS

DAILY TASKS

"*I do not try to please everyone.*"

DAILY GOALS

DAILY TASKS

Self-Care Saturday

CHECK THE BOXES OF THE ACTIVITIES YOU DO TO TAKE CARE OF YOURSELF.

- ☐ EAT THREE MAIN MEALS
- ☐ GO ON A 24-HOUR SOCIAL MEDIA DETOX
- ☐ FIND A QUIET SPOT TO MEDITATE
- ☐ LIGHT AN AROMATIC CANDLE
- ☐ DO A GRATITUDE LIST
- ☐ PRACTICE DEEP BREATHING
- ☐ LISTEN TO GOOD MUSIC
- ☐ EXERCISE
- ☐ CATCH UP WITH A FRIEND
- ☐ VISIT A FAMILY MEMBER
- ☐ SPEND TIME OUTDOORS
- ☐ HAVE A MINI PAMPER SESSION
- ☐ CUDDLE A PET
- ☐ TRY SOMETHING NEW
- ☐ READ A BOOK

Make it a habit to take care of yourself!

THIS WEEK

I AM GRATEFUL FOR

"My family holds a special place in my heart."

"Actions prove who I am, words just prove who I want to be."

"Because I have only one life to live, I live it with no regrets."

DAILY GOALS

DAILY TASKS

"I am imperfectly perfect."

"I do not hold grudges."

DAILY GOALS

DAILY TASKS

"Even on hard days, I know that better days are coming."

Self-Care Saturday

CHECK THE BOXES OF THE ACTIVITIES YOU DO TO TAKE CARE OF YOURSELF.

- ⬜ EAT THREE MAIN MEALS
- ⬜ GO ON A 24-HOUR SOCIAL MEDIA DETOX
- ⬜ FIND A QUIET SPOT TO MEDITATE
- ⬜ LIGHT AN AROMATIC CANDLE
- ⬜ DO A GRATITUDE LIST
- ⬜ PRACTICE DEEP BREATHING
- ⬜ LISTEN TO GOOD MUSIC
- ⬜ EXERCISE
- ⬜ CATCH UP WITH A FRIEND
- ⬜ VISIT A FAMILY MEMBER
- ⬜ SPEND TIME OUTDOORS
- ⬜ HAVE A MINI PAMPER SESSION
- ⬜ CUDDLE A PET
- ⬜ TRY SOMETHING NEW
- ⬜ READ A BOOK

Make it a habit to take care of yourself!

THIS WEEK

I AM GRATEFUL FOR

"I am resilient."

DAILY GOALS

DAILY TASKS

"I repent of my sins daily."

> *"I owe myself the love that I so freely give to others."*

DAILY GOALS

DAILY TASKS

"I begin and go throughout my day with an 'I get to' mentality rather than a 'I have to' mentality."

"I will do it now. There are only so many tomorrows."

"Everything I am going through is preparing me for what I asked for."

____

____

____

____

____

____

____

DAILY GOALS

○
○
○

DAILY TASKS

○
○
○

Self-Care Saturday

- EAT THREE MAIN MEALS
- GO ON A 24-HOUR SOCIAL MEDIA DETOX
- FIND A QUIET SPOT TO MEDITATE
- LIGHT AN AROMATIC CANDLE
- DO A GRATITUDE LIST
- PRACTICE DEEP BREATHING
- LISTEN TO GOOD MUSIC
- EXERCISE
- CATCH UP WITH A FRIEND
- VISIT A FAMILY MEMBER
- SPEND TIME OUTDOORS
- HAVE A MINI PAMPER SESSION
- CUDDLE A PET
- TRY SOMETHING NEW
- READ A BOOK

Make it a habit to take care of yourself!

THIS WEEK

I AM GRATEFUL FOR

> # *"As long as I am breathing, I am blessed."*

_______________________________________ ○
_______________________________________ ○
_______________________________________ ○

_______________________________________ ○
_______________________________________ ○
_______________________________________ ○

"Everything in life is temporary."

DAILY GOALS

DAILY TASKS

"The only difference between where you are and where you want to be is the steps you haven't taken yet." -Rigel J. Dawson

Monthly PLANNER

SUN	MON	TUE	WED

JUL

AUG

SEP

OCT

NOV

DEC   YEAR ________________

THU	FRI	SAT	NOTES

"I never know what I can or cannot do until I try."

"I use the talents and abilities God has given me to develop as fully as I can."

"I maximize the power that is within me."

____

____

____

____

____

____

____

DAILY GOALS

DAILY TASKS

____

"I prioritize myself."

____

____

____

____

____

____

____

____

DAILY GOALS

_______________________________________ ◯

_______________________________________ ◯

_______________________________________ ◯

DAILY TASKS

_______________________________________ ◯

_______________________________________ ◯

_______________________________________ ◯

"I trust my instincts."

DAILY GOALS

DAILY TASKS

"I am not afraid to say 'yes'."

____

____

____

____

____

____

____

DAILY GOALS

____ ◯

____ ◯

____ ◯

DAILY TASKS

____ ◯

____ ◯

____ ◯

"I listen to understand, not to respond."

Self-Care Saturday

CHECK THE BOXES OF THE ACTIVITIES YOU DO TO TAKE CARE OF YOURSELF.

- ◯ EAT THREE MAIN MEALS
- ◯ GO ON A 24-HOUR SOCIAL MEDIA DETOX
- ◯ FIND A QUIET SPOT TO MEDITATE
- ◯ LIGHT AN AROMATIC CANDLE
- ◯ DO A GRATITUDE LIST
- ◯ PRACTICE DEEP BREATHING
- ◯ LISTEN TO GOOD MUSIC
- ◯ EXERCISE
- ◯ CATCH UP WITH A FRIEND
- ◯ VISIT A FAMILY MEMBER
- ◯ SPEND TIME OUTDOORS
- ◯ HAVE A MINI PAMPER SESSION
- ◯ CUDDLE A PET
- ◯ TRY SOMETHING NEW
- ◯ READ A BOOK

Make it a habit to take care of yourself!

THIS WEEK

I AM GRATEFUL FOR

"I do not owe anyone anything."

DAILY GOALS

DAILY TASKS

"I am irreplaceable."

____

____

____

____

____

____

____

DAILY GOALS

___________________________ ○
___________________________ ○
___________________________ ○

DAILY TASKS

___________________________ ○
___________________________ ○
___________________________ ○

"I am special."

"I have motivating friends."

____

____

____

____

____

____

____

"I live a balanced life."

DAILY GOALS

DAILY TASKS

Self-Care Saturday

CHECK THE BOXES OF THE ACTIVITIES YOU DO TO TAKE CARE OF YOURSELF.

- ☐ EAT THREE MAIN MEALS
- ☐ GO ON A 24-HOUR SOCIAL MEDIA DETOX
- ☐ FIND A QUIET SPOT TO MEDITATE
- ☐ LIGHT AN AROMATIC CANDLE
- ☐ DO A GRATITUDE LIST
- ☐ PRACTICE DEEP BREATHING
- ☐ LISTEN TO GOOD MUSIC
- ☐ EXERCISE
- ☐ CATCH UP WITH A FRIEND
- ☐ VISIT A FAMILY MEMBER
- ☐ SPEND TIME OUTDOORS
- ☐ HAVE A MINI PAMPER SESSION
- ☐ CUDDLE A PET
- ☐ TRY SOMETHING NEW
- ☐ READ A BOOK

Make it a habit to take care of yourself!

THIS WEEK

I AM GRATEFUL FOR

"I do not fear failure."

"I understand the value of my voice."

DAILY GOALS

DAILY TASKS

"I will not allow worry to rob me of my destiny."

DAILY GOALS

DAILY TASKS

____

____

____

____

____

____

____

DAILY GOALS

DAILY TASKS

DAILY GOALS

DAILY TASKS

"I was given this life because I am strong enough to live it."

Self-Care
Saturday

CHECK THE BOXES OF THE ACTIVITIES YOU DO TO TAKE CARE OF YOURSELF.

- ⬭ EAT THREE MAIN MEALS
- ⬭ GO ON A 24-HOUR SOCIAL MEDIA DETOX
- ⬭ FIND A QUIET SPOT TO MEDITATE
- ⬭ LIGHT AN AROMATIC CANDLE
- ⬭ DO A GRATITUDE LIST
- ⬭ PRACTICE DEEP BREATHING
- ⬭ LISTEN TO GOOD MUSIC
- ⬭ EXERCISE
- ⬭ CATCH UP WITH A FRIEND
- ⬭ VISIT A FAMILY MEMBER
- ⬭ SPEND TIME OUTDOORS
- ⬭ HAVE A MINI PAMPER SESSION
- ⬭ CUDDLE A PET
- ⬭ TRY SOMETHING NEW
- ⬭ READ A BOOK

Make it a habit to take care of yourself!

THIS WEEK

I AM GRATEFUL FOR

"I am planted, but not buried."

DAILY GOALS

DAILY TASKS

"God is turning my 'mess' into a message
and that 'test' into a testimony."

____

____

____

____

____

____

____

DAILY GOALS

○
○
○

DAILY TASKS

○
○
○

"I have destroyed the idea that there is an expectation to do things by a certain age."

DAILY GOALS

DAILY TASKS

"I see my full potential."

DAILY GOALS

DAILY TASKS

"There will always be a reason why you meet people. Either you need them to change your life, or you're the one that will change theirs."
-Angel Flonis Harefa

"I am stable."

"I take full responsibility for my actions."

Self-Care Saturday

- ☐ EAT THREE MAIN MEALS
- ☐ GO ON A 24-HOUR SOCIAL MEDIA DETOX
- ☐ FIND A QUIET SPOT TO MEDITATE
- ☐ LIGHT AN AROMATIC CANDLE
- ☐ DO A GRATITUDE LIST
- ☐ PRACTICE DEEP BREATHING
- ☐ LISTEN TO GOOD MUSIC
- ☐ EXERCISE
- ☐ CATCH UP WITH A FRIEND
- ☐ VISIT A FAMILY MEMBER
- ☐ SPEND TIME OUTDOORS
- ☐ HAVE A MINI PAMPER SESSION
- ☐ CUDDLE A PET
- ☐ TRY SOMETHING NEW
- ☐ READ A BOOK

Make it a habit to take care of yourself!

THIS WEEK

I AM GRATEFUL FOR

"I do not live in shame."

"I am obedient."

____

____

____

____

____

____

____

DAILY GOALS

_______________________ ◻

_______________________ ◻

_______________________ ◻

DAILY TASKS

_______________________ ◻

_______________________ ◻

_______________________ ◻

"I extend grace to others."

DAILY GOALS

DAILY TASKS

Self care is THE best care! Have you completed any self care activities lately?

Monthly PLANNER

SUN	MON	TUE	WED

<u>Worship Song of the Month</u>
"The Blessing" by Kari Jobe, Cody Carnes, and Elevation Worship

THU	FRI	SAT	NOTES

"I serve people well."

____

____

____

____

____

____

____

DAILY GOALS

____ ◯

____ ◯

____ ◯

DAILY TASKS

____ ◯

____ ◯

____ ◯

"I am understanding."

"I am living/walking in my purpose."

____

____

____

____

____

____

____

DAILY GOALS

DAILY TASKS

"I am creative."

DAILY GOALS

DAILY TASKS

"I can speak for myself."

"My voice is heard."

____

____

____

____

____

____

____

DAILY GOALS

○

○

○

DAILY TASKS

○

○

○

DAILY GOALS

DAILY TASKS

Self-Care Saturday

CHECK THE BOXES OF THE ACTIVITIES YOU DO TO TAKE CARE OF YOURSELF.

- ☐ EAT THREE MAIN MEALS
- ☐ GO ON A 24-HOUR SOCIAL MEDIA DETOX
- ☐ FIND A QUIET SPOT TO MEDITATE
- ☐ LIGHT AN AROMATIC CANDLE
- ☐ DO A GRATITUDE LIST
- ☐ PRACTICE DEEP BREATHING
- ☐ LISTEN TO GOOD MUSIC
- ☐ EXERCISE
- ☐ CATCH UP WITH A FRIEND
- ☐ VISIT A FAMILY MEMBER
- ☐ SPEND TIME OUTDOORS
- ☐ HAVE A MINI PAMPER SESSION
- ☐ CUDDLE A PET
- ☐ TRY SOMETHING NEW
- ☐ READ A BOOK

Make it a habit to take care of yourself!

THIS WEEK

I AM GRATEFUL FOR

"I tithe regularly."

DAILY GOALS

DAILY TASKS

"I am grateful for my source(s) of income."

____

____

____

____

____

____

____

DAILY GOALS

DAILY TASKS

"I am generous."

DAILY GOALS

DAILY TASKS

"I am a cheerful giver."

"Pride does not live within me."

DAILY GOALS

DAILY TASKS

"I am an observant person."

____

____

____

____

____

____

____

DAILY GOALS

_______________________________ ☐
_______________________________ ☐
_______________________________ ☐

DAILY TASKS

_______________________________ ☐
_______________________________ ☐
_______________________________ ☐

Self-Care Saturday

CHECK THE BOXES OF THE ACTIVITIES YOU DO TO TAKE CARE OF YOURSELF.

- [ ] EAT THREE MAIN MEALS
- [ ] GO ON A 24-HOUR SOCIAL MEDIA DETOX
- [ ] FIND A QUIET SPOT TO MEDITATE
- [ ] LIGHT AN AROMATIC CANDLE
- [ ] DO A GRATITUDE LIST
- [ ] PRACTICE DEEP BREATHING
- [ ] LISTEN TO GOOD MUSIC
- [ ] EXERCISE
- [ ] CATCH UP WITH A FRIEND
- [ ] VISIT A FAMILY MEMBER
- [ ] SPEND TIME OUTDOORS
- [ ] HAVE A MINI PAMPER SESSION
- [ ] CUDDLE A PET
- [ ] TRY SOMETHING NEW
- [ ] READ A BOOK

Make it a habit to take care of yourself!

THIS WEEK

I AM GRATEFUL FOR

"I am a great listener."

"I am open to new ideas."

"*I live in a state of expectancy.*"

"_I am a reliable person._"

DAILY GOALS

DAILY TASKS

"Sometimes [my] circle decreases in size, but increases in value." -Dulce Ruby

DAILY GOALS

DAILY TASKS

"I have great communication skills."

____

____

____

____

____

____

____

____

DAILY GOALS

____ ☐
____ ☐
____ ☐

DAILY TASKS

____ ☐
____ ☐
____ ☐

"I stand tall in my truth."

Self-Care Saturday

CHECK THE BOXES OF THE ACTIVITIES YOU DO TO TAKE CARE OF YOURSELF.

- ◯ EAT THREE MAIN MEALS
- ◯ GO ON A 24-HOUR SOCIAL MEDIA DETOX
- ◯ FIND A QUIET SPOT TO MEDITATE
- ◯ LIGHT AN AROMATIC CANDLE
- ◯ DO A GRATITUDE LIST
- ◯ PRACTICE DEEP BREATHING
- ◯ LISTEN TO GOOD MUSIC
- ◯ EXERCISE
- ◯ CATCH UP WITH A FRIEND
- ◯ VISIT A FAMILY MEMBER
- ◯ SPEND TIME OUTDOORS
- ◯ HAVE A MINI PAMPER SESSION
- ◯ CUDDLE A PET
- ◯ TRY SOMETHING NEW
- ◯ READ A BOOK

Make it a habit to take care of yourself!

THIS WEEK

I AM GRATEFUL FOR

DAILY GOALS

DAILY TASKS

"I am a straightforward person."

"If I am unsure about something, my first instinct is to ask about it."

DAILY GOALS

DAILY TASKS

"I use my energy wisely."

DAILY GOALS

DAILY TASKS

____

____

____

____

____

____

____

DAILY GOALS

_______________________________________ ☐
_______________________________________ ☐
_______________________________________ ☐

DAILY TASKS

_______________________________________ ☐
_______________________________________ ☐
_______________________________________ ☐

"God is working out things I have not prayed for yet."

"It is safe to love again."

____

____

____

____

____

____

____

DAILY GOALS

_______________________________________ ○
_______________________________________ ○
_______________________________________ ○

DAILY TASKS

_______________________________________ ○
_______________________________________ ○
_______________________________________ ○

THIS WEEK
I AM GRATEFUL FOR

"I love and accept myself in spite of my imperfections."

"I am no longer attached to anything that keeps me stagnant."

Monthly PLANNER

SUN	MON	TUE	WED

<u>Worship Song of the Month</u>
"Greater is Coming"
by Jekalyn Carr

THU	FRI	SAT	NOTES

Quarterly Accountability

What do you want to accomplish over this quarter?

What did you actually accomplish?

DAILY GOALS

DAILY TASKS

DAILY GOALS

DAILY TASKS

DAILY GOALS

DAILY TASKS

"I treat people with dignity and respect."

DAILY GOALS

DAILY TASKS

"I do not expect all of my blessings to be financial or materialistic."

"I build in silence."

"I will not give up on the person I am becoming."

Self-Care Saturday

CHECK THE BOXES OF THE ACTIVITIES YOU DO TO TAKE CARE OF YOURSELF.

- ☐ EAT THREE MAIN MEALS
- ☐ GO ON A 24-HOUR SOCIAL MEDIA DETOX
- ☐ FIND A QUIET SPOT TO MEDITATE
- ☐ LIGHT AN AROMATIC CANDLE
- ☐ DO A GRATITUDE LIST
- ☐ PRACTICE DEEP BREATHING
- ☐ LISTEN TO GOOD MUSIC
- ☐ EXERCISE
- ☐ CATCH UP WITH A FRIEND
- ☐ VISIT A FAMILY MEMBER
- ☐ SPEND TIME OUTDOORS
- ☐ HAVE A MINI PAMPER SESSION
- ☐ CUDDLE A PET
- ☐ TRY SOMETHING NEW
- ☐ READ A BOOK

Make it a habit to take care of yourself!

THIS WEEK
I AM GRATEFUL FOR

"It is the repetition of affirmations
that lead to belief."

____

____

____

____

____

____

____

DAILY GOALS

_______________________________ ☐
_______________________________ ☐
_______________________________ ☐

DAILY TASKS

_______________________________ ☐
_______________________________ ☐
_______________________________ ☐

DAILY GOALS

DAILY TASKS

DAILY GOALS

DAILY TASKS

> # "I pray on it, over it, and through it."

____

"I receive the fruits of my labor."

____

____

____

____

____

____

____

____

DAILY GOALS

○

○

○

DAILY TASKS

○

○

○

"I have evolved from my old ways."

____

____

____

____

____

____

____

Self-Care Saturday

CHECK THE BOXES OF THE ACTIVITIES YOU DO TO TAKE CARE OF YOURSELF.

- ◯ EAT THREE MAIN MEALS
- ◯ GO ON A 24-HOUR SOCIAL MEDIA DETOX
- ◯ FIND A QUIET SPOT TO MEDITATE
- ◯ LIGHT AN AROMATIC CANDLE
- ◯ DO A GRATITUDE LIST
- ◯ PRACTICE DEEP BREATHING
- ◯ LISTEN TO GOOD MUSIC
- ◯ EXERCISE
- ◯ CATCH UP WITH A FRIEND
- ◯ VISIT A FAMILY MEMBER
- ◯ SPEND TIME OUTDOORS
- ◯ HAVE A MINI PAMPER SESSION
- ◯ CUDDLE A PET
- ◯ TRY SOMETHING NEW
- ◯ READ A BOOK

Make it a habit to take care of yourself!

THIS WEEK

I AM GRATEFUL FOR

"*I am thankful for rejections.*"

DAILY GOALS

DAILY TASKS

"I do not look like what I have been through."

____

____

____

____

____

____

____

DAILY GOALS

DAILY TASKS

DAILY GOALS

DAILY TASKS

DAILY GOALS

DAILY TASKS

"I make decisions from my heart."

DAILY GOALS

DAILY TASKS

DAILY GOALS

DAILY TASKS

"I do not have resentment towards anyone."

DAILY GOALS

DAILY TASKS

Self-Care Saturday

CHECK THE BOXES OF THE ACTIVITIES YOU DO TO TAKE CARE OF YOURSELF.

- ☐ EAT THREE MAIN MEALS
- ☐ GO ON A 24-HOUR SOCIAL MEDIA DETOX
- ☐ FIND A QUIET SPOT TO MEDITATE
- ☐ LIGHT AN AROMATIC CANDLE
- ☐ DO A GRATITUDE LIST
- ☐ PRACTICE DEEP BREATHING
- ☐ LISTEN TO GOOD MUSIC
- ☐ EXERCISE
- ☐ CATCH UP WITH A FRIEND
- ☐ VISIT A FAMILY MEMBER
- ☐ SPEND TIME OUTDOORS
- ☐ HAVE A MINI PAMPER SESSION
- ☐ CUDDLE A PET
- ☐ TRY SOMETHING NEW
- ☐ READ A BOOK

Make it a habit to take care of yourself!

THIS WEEK

I AM GRATEFUL FOR

"Love always wins."

DAILY GOALS

DAILY TASKS

"God is using what I have been through to strengthen me."

DAILY GOALS

DAILY TASKS

"I am prepared for new beginnings."

"No matter how hard life is, [I] go to bed grateful [I] still have one." -Kristen Butler

"I am going places my resume does not qualify me for."

DAILY GOALS

DAILY TASKS

"I will not bring the old version of me into a new season."

DAILY GOALS

DAILY TASKS

"Nobody has me like God does."

Self-Care Saturday

CHECK THE BOXES OF THE ACTIVITIES YOU DO TO TAKE CARE OF YOURSELF.

- ◯ EAT THREE MAIN MEALS
- ◯ GO ON A 24-HOUR SOCIAL MEDIA DETOX
- ◯ FIND A QUIET SPOT TO MEDITATE
- ◯ LIGHT AN AROMATIC CANDLE
- ◯ DO A GRATITUDE LIST
- ◯ PRACTICE DEEP BREATHING
- ◯ LISTEN TO GOOD MUSIC
- ◯ EXERCISE
- ◯ CATCH UP WITH A FRIEND
- ◯ VISIT A FAMILY MEMBER
- ◯ SPEND TIME OUTDOORS
- ◯ HAVE A MINI PAMPER SESSION
- ◯ CUDDLE A PET
- ◯ TRY SOMETHING NEW
- ◯ READ A BOOK

Make it a habit to take care of yourself!

THIS WEEK

I AM GRATEFUL FOR

"I welcome change with an open heart and mind."

DAILY GOALS

DAILY TASKS

"My personality is unique; no one has one like it."

DAILY GOALS

DAILY TASKS

"I pray bold prayers."

CPSIA information can be obtained
at www.ICGtesting.com
Printed in the USA
BVHW010441060721
611221BV00013B/783